Just- For- Fun- Poetry Two

Camille Kay Bogle

Copyright© 2020 By James A Bogle
All rights reserved. Use of any materials or artwork found in this book is prohibited.
ISBN: 978-1-7322793-1-5

All Poems by Camille Kay Bogle

Cover design by James A Bogle
Cover Artwork "Spring Time In Texas"
By James A Bogle

Edited by James A Bogle

Special thanks to

Nita Feliciano

This Book Is Dedicated To My Sons

Don Cameron Bogle
William Brett Bogle
James Allison Bogle
John Barry Bogle

Table of Contents

Autobiographically Speaking

Let's Face It 6
"Make It A Double" Celebration 7
When I Get To Be-Ah, Older 8
Half And Half 9
Answer This 10
Maybe Not 11
Riding High 12
Paradise Found 13
Do You Promise? 14
Word–y 15
Traditionally Speaking 16
In A Word 17
Wisely Put 18
Let's Muse 19

Philosophy 101 And Sense

It's Called Now 20
A Timely Act 21
Bubble – Wrap- It 22
Call It Gamesmanship 23

Call It Fun 24
Can You Game It? 26
Try It 27
Simply Said 28
Side-Lines 29
A Friend Indeed.. 30
It's a recipe 31
It's Collateral 32
Full Of Wonder...33
Here's To Our Fourth Of July 34

Flowers and Nonsense

Texas In Springtime 35
Say it with Flowers 36
Flower Potting 37
Garden Variety 38
I Surrender 39
Who's Asking? 40
What's The Question 41
Here's Telling You "Y"..................................42
Chess, Any One? 43
Hello, New Year 44
Resolution Time 45
New Year's Time Again 46
It's Gotta Be Love 47
Love is The First Step 48
Sign Up Here! 49

Let's Face It

I love getting letters
So I write letters quite a bit.
It's a habit I keep easily–
Want others to practice it !

Like the art of conversation
Shouldn't be reduced to a text.
I will keep my phone working,
And be sure neighbors come next.

The world runs on communication,
Both on earth and in outer space,
But the best close encounter.
Is when we talk face to face !

"Make It A Double" Celebration!

It's always National "something" Day
On the date that you were born
So that's a double reason
For you to toot your horn.

And you can also bet
It's some famous person's special date.
There's a long list to check out,
And it's always fun to celebrate.

It's on December Fifteenth
That I always toot my horn.
It is also I'm proud to say
When the Bill of Rights was born!

When I Get To Be-Ah, Older

I'm not blowing out any candles –
I can surely tell you that!
I'm never going on a diet,
So forget about Low-Fat.

I may decide to dye my hair –
Perhaps a flaming red,
And I want no one asking
Is that someone in your bed?

I want to think there's mystery
So life stays a lot of fun.
I may give up the skiing,
But not my place in the sun.

So as to Act-Your-Age advice,
Of that I want no part!
I'm staying a Charter Member
Of that club called "Young At Heart"!

Half And Half

Trying to overcome inertia
Is really never ever easy.
It takes all of my gumption–
Never works if I feel " queasy",

Sometimes it's lovely to do nothing-
I'll just leave it at that.
It may be fun to be a spectator,
Letting others go up to bat.

You can be a saint or a sinner,
If it's all about the fame,
I guess I'm somewhere in the middle
Half sweetheart and half "dame".

Answer This

When morning comes around,
What gets you out of bed?
First, check the weather,
Maybe coffee first instead.

It's not a coincidence
I'm going to work I love.
It's useful, on going and fun,
Yes, all of the above.

It takes people by the millions
To run this planet Earth.
So many pieces to the puzzle,
It's hard to measure one man's worth.

My faith keeps me going,
I believe with all my heart-
The world will keep on turning
If I just do my part!

Maybe Not

The "Things-I-might-never- do "List
Gets longer day by day.
The Great Wall of China doesn't interest me,
It's something I once did really say.

After due consideration,
I added Mount Everest to the list.
I rode a Gondola in Las Vegas,
So visiting Venice can be missed.

I've already seen the Sahara,
Nothing appealing about the Gobi.
From the Eifel Tower, I saw Paris
No hot air balloons for me.

I suppose as I get older,
I like to travel vicariously,
I am thrilled that I didn't miss
This era of videos and TV!

Riding High

I rode a camel in Egypt;
My boat ride came with a crew.
I even once rode an elephant
When visiting the Houston zoo.

The local amusement park
Gave me a pony ride.
I love flying in an airplane
Getting to sit by the pilot's side.

I rented a donkey in Libya.
It was an adventurous thing to do.
And when it comes to horses,
I've ridden more than a few.

While up in a balloon,
We looked out over the sea,
But one ride I'm too scared to take-
That roller coaster can do without me!

Paradise Found

We all love our lanai,
It's a bower of green,
A lovely walk to the patio,
Off and on flowers are seen.

Now we have two parrots,
Adding color to the walk.
We don't even mind,
They never seem to talk.

There's a big rooftop terrace,
One can see the ocean from there.
We can see the stars come out,
While enjoying the night-time air.

We make our own Piña Coladas:
We say they are worth the price.
It's called a land of enchantment,
We call Puerto Rico paradise.

Do You Promise?

Instead of New Year's resolutions,
Counting blessing is my gig.
I will start off with the small ones,
But some are pretty big.

God bless the world-wide farmers
Millions of people have to be fed.
We put our trust in builders
To put that roof over each one's head.

Knowing how to connect the wires
Is a profession and a trade.
Technology is all about connections,
And how the future will be made.

But mostly I am blessed
I can live without much strife
Above all, I'm incredibly thankful,
To have a loving family in my life.

Word-y

If you are in love with words,
You are called a logophile.
I prefer the title poet –
It has a lot more style.

One label is a wordsmith,
Perhaps that says it all;
And we do not like labels,
But you can't escape short or tall.

No one wants to be put in a box
And please don't categorize-
The best of just about anything,
Can come in any shape or size.

But you can call me poet, -
Since I answer most to that,
And if I do not answer,
Well, I'm just wearing a different hat!

Traditionally Speaking

There is an old Tradition
One that we hold dear.
You have to love black-eyed peas.
To give good luck to this New Year!

To go with this tradition,
Corn bread must make the list.
Hot from the oven with butter.
A treat not to be missed.

So come in and sit a spell.
There's at least a taste for you.
Of black-eyed peas and corn bread
So that you can be lucky too!

In A Word

When it's pretty awesome,
I'll give it a tip o' the hat.
If I call it a HUMDINGER,
It's much more than that.

People seem stuck on some words
Myself, I'm giving up "wall".
It seems like "security"
Should serve and say it all.

And you can call me "babe",
I like pet names a lot.
If you're looking for trouble,.
Surely trouble is what you got.

The saying "words can't hurt me",
Was invented for a reason.
Sometimes semantics are just nonsense,
Let's call it the "silly season".

Fashions always come and go,
It just takes a while.
The day is surely coming
The "PC" will be out of style.

Wisely Put

I'm not a put-it-off person
My nature is to do it now.
Of course, there's a next step.
I've got to figure out "how".

We all have our puzzles;
Problem-solving is the essence of living.
One part is our gifts received,
To balance what we are giving.

What truly makes us happy
May sometimes take us by surprise.
The trick is to enjoy the moments.
It sure is great, to be wise!

Let's Muse

I love the life I've lived
I did follow my heart.
I thank my lucky genes.
That gave me a head start.

Any regret I can dream up,
I have to think a bit.
I didn't learn to fly a plane,
But my partner was a perfect fit.

We both loved to see the world,
Some of the seven seas as well,
It was fun to live in many places
Ah, the stories I have to tell.

But now I please myself,
I no longer want to roam.
I love my memories and one spot.
Now there's no place like home!

It's Called Now

You could say I'm of vintage age
It depends on your taste
It comes with a proviso—
There's no time to waste.

You'll never do it at all
If you don't do it now.
My best friend told me that
It's true oh boy, and how,

So at this vintage age of life,
I think I'll take my ease.
Now has a new meaning—
It's called " do as you please."

A Timely Act

Time sure flies by
Whether you're having fun or not.
One question comes to mind;
How much time have I got?

Some people just drift along,
While other go too deep.
Maybe you've heard this-
Have faith and just leap.

This is the time to do it.
Choose your path and take it.
Stick to those things you like-
Life is really what you make it.

Bubble-Wrap-It

The world is too much with us
There's news and noise on every side,
With multimedia at full throttle,
There's just no where to hide.

Everyone should create a bubble,
That shuts out scenes and sounds.
Fill it up with what you like,
And people that you want around.

Let's call it "filter living" —
Only positive things get through.
Having set out the formula,
The rest is positively up to you!

Call It Gamesmanship

Since every life is a work-in-progress,
Don't let "stuff" worry you.
You'll know what makes you happy,
The things you like to do.

As the seasons come and go,
Usually moods do the same,
Decide that you will master
Just how to play the game.

It may be good to score points,
Just keep up the play.
Make sure to move forward
Often times you'll win the day.

It helps to assemble your team,
With people who really like to run,
It's a great time for celebration,
If the score board just reads "fun"!

Call It Fun

I can't remember when
It was such a long time ago.
I stopped caring what others think,
It's a waste of time, you know.

Just consider it noise-
And what you prefer not to hear.
It's great to have a filter system,
I've had mine for many a year.

It's the only way to live,
Doing what you want to do.
I even say what I think,
And I hope you do, too.

We'll have to agree,
We just have to get along.
The main lesson to learn
Is telling which are right from wrong.

Doctors have it as "Doc-trine";
To others, do no harm.
It's OK to like city lights,
And others will choose to farm.

Everyone has some challenges,
Problems both small and large,
Often saying, "'twould be better",
If I was just in charge.

P.S.

Now I'm working on my patience
Can't help my philosophy-
Yes, 'twould be a better world.
If it was left up to me!

Can You Game It?

Have a land of second chances?
Yes, one should never give up.
Fighting that every day battles.
Well, it isn't a world cup.

If you don't ever try,
The chance may be lost.
The game just got started–
The coin only just tossed.

To say words like "giving up"
Are unworthy of one's name.
Life is always and forever
About how you play the game!

Try It

You have to try to connect
If you want people to do their best.
If it comes to you naturally
You are well and truly blessed.

But you should know this–
It's a skill to be learned.
It will be quite rewarding,
You'll soon reap what you've earned

The world needs this positive energy,
And you can do your part.
It also comes with a bonus,
Your own happy healthy heart!

Simply Said

My solution may sound simple,
But "stuff" does accumulate,
It takes real determination
To achieve that simple state.

Have faith within yourself,
And listen to your heart.
Let God take care of Big Things,
Just do your own small part.

Worry is a waste of time,
It steals your very soul.
Create and enjoy Life's beauty,
Make Happiness your goal!

Side –Lines

While the mind rules willpower,
Gumption takes a lot of guts.
While we admire thoroughbreds,
We fall in love with mutts.

Comparisons actually do a job,
They force us to measure.
We all hear that trash,
Can be another man's treasure.

So the two party system
Is a method to celebrate.
Most things have two sides,
If you want a great debate.

It has taken millenniums
To bring about America's birth.
We're all in this together—
Let's Take care of Mother Earth.

A Friend, Indeed

A real treasure in life
Is to have a good friend,
One you can always count on
To be there to the end.

As time goes by, one learns
That such a person is rare.
So nonchalant when young
Seeming too busy to care.

However there's one other thing,
That I have to append.
It may be the most rewarding,
Just being that good friend!

It's A Recipe

A recipe for the best in cooking,
Should always be the same,
But that recipe for life
Needs variety in the game.

Sometimes it can be simple,
With intervals of rest.
Other times, should be a challenge,
Putting talents to the test.

Know what you do not want,
Then decide " that's for me!"
The goal is being able to say
There's nobody I'd rather be.

Being happy really is an option,
But you do have to believe it.
Now, the where, with who, and how
Is up to you to achieve it.

It's Collateral

Age does come with collateral perks,
Whether they are deserved or not,
But don't take them for granted,
Say "thank you", quite a lot.

Now as to collateral damage,
(A by-product, it's true)
If you are accident prone,
I'm definitely talking to you.

Watch your every, single step.
Beware at each and every stage.
It will result, collaterally of course,
In your reaching a good "old age"!

Full Of Wonder

This old world is so big,
There is a lot to wonder about.
It's hard to know where to start–
Don't want to leave much out.

The sun, moon, and stars,
Will we say "Heaven's Above?"
There's faith, hope, and charity,
The greatest thing is love.

Some things are taken for granted,
Perhaps one of these is health,
It is the best of good fortune,
And greater than any wealth.

Just to be born is a miracle,
And to live in a place of peace.
But best is having curiosity,
"May Wonders Never Cease"!

Here's To Our Fourth Of July!

I love the Fourth of July.
It thrills my American heart!
A time for us to celebrate
A glorious and joyous date–
Each pledging to do one's part.

To cherish our words of freedom
And proud heritage so grand;
A history to learn,
A commitment to earn
And keep this wonderful land!

Each new generation has a job
To plan and forge the way.
Our great future, you see,
Is the one that can be–
Only MADE IN THE USA!

Texas In Springtime

I mostly dream of Texas
When bluebonnets are in bloom,
And I have these lovely blossoms
In a picture in my room.

Sometimes there is a place,
That sets itself apart.
So bluebonnets in Texas
Keep a place in my heart.

Mixed with Indian Paint Brush,
Both flowers like a sea—
Making a colorful carpet
To transport us — you and me.

Spring is the promise of renewal,
Dispelling gloom and doom.
Ah, to be in Texas,
When bluebonnets start to bloom!

Saying It With Flowers

Periwinkles and Zinnias
Make a garden bright.
Hyacinth and Larkspur
Are also a pretty sight.

Did you notice that Wisteria
Hangs around all the time?
And Impatiens hang in baskets,
While Bougainvillea loves to climb.

Geraniums are very hardy;
They can always take the heat.
For another touch of color,
Marigolds are hard to beat.

I love the smell of Jasmine
Sweetening the night-time air,
And there's nothing like a Hibiscus
For showing off the hair.

Among Nature's greatest blessings
Are the Flowers that bloom in May.
If variety is the spice of life,
It also makes a GREAT BOUQUET!

Flower-Plotting

When laying out a garden
Put some humor in the task.
If you then have any questions,
You only have to ask.
I've often heard that Peonies
Are rather hard to grow,
And Camellias are sometimes rare –
Of that I happen to know.

But velvety, little Pansies
Are lovely to the touch,
And don't forget Petunias
That everyone loves so much.
The dainty, little Buttercup
In its meadow it should stay,
And we all know a Primrose path
Can lead anyone astray.

If you like Honeysuckle,
It makes a pretty vine,
And even Dandelions are good
If you want to make some wine.
But what is the favorite flower
That in the garden grows?
Surely every gardener wants
At least one lovely, fragrant Rose!

Garden Variety

Everyone loves Gardenias,
And Lilies in the pond.
Of Iris and Sunflowers,
Artists are very fond.

The Violet shrinks too much;
The Morning Glory seems too shy;
Birds of Paradise too stately;
And Carnations take to dye.

A Daisy can be fragile,
And Glads are rather stiff.
There are Daffodils and Jonquils,
But who can tell the diff.

It's hard to wear a Tulip,
Despite what's said in song,
And it's not very often
That Apple Blossom come along.

If you are giving me Flowers,
I hope you read my mind!
Since everyone gets Roses,
An Orchid suits me just fine!

I Surrender

Some things are irresistible
Have a magnetism of their own.
It's true of special friends,
Certain people I have known.

On some days of the year,
Doughnuts and chocolate qualify,
When barbeque is in the air,
Just eat, don't question why.

Temptations do just come and go,
Particularly that celebration cup–
I call it that "Movable Object",
It's time to say "I Give Up!"

Who's asking?

Someone is always asking
What weekday is today?
Think what was on TV last night,

Then I can usually say–
But re-runs have messed me up–
Tho' I still know what year.
The easiest question is where are you?
Because I'm always right here.

I'll keep my sense of humor
Until the sweet bye and bye.
And especially when anyone asks me
"Can you tell me who am I?"

What's The Question?

When asked what day it is,
If I cared, I might know.
I know when it is Tuesday,
'Cause I watch a special show.

A calendar was invented,
Not leaving things to chance-
It's good to keep appointments
I don't want to miss the dance.

I don't really mind reminders.
Great for keeping on the go,
And I might have my fun asking,
Just why do you want to know?

Here's Telling You "Y"

When you come to Norman's "Y",
You can do quite a lot.
There's exercise and swimming;
You can trek or walk or trot.

It is all really up to you.
It's not one thing fits all.
You'll see all shapes and sizes,
Plus the short and very tall.

We hope you'll join in the fun
And get healthier to boot.
This "Y" is quite the greatest,
And a holler and a hoot.

We admit some facts are painful,
But this much is surely true:
There'll be "someone else" a-tryin'
To lose a lot more than you!

Chess, anyone?

After a lot of study,
I'm still not great at chess.
The more I learn about it,
I end up knowing less.

Knight moves can be different —
As different as (k)night and day,
So I decided to vacation
And get really far away.

I ended up in Australia;
You could say that it was fate.
I took new friends to dinner —
I could FINALLY say, "CHECK! MATE!"

Hello New Year!

Saying "Happy New Year"
Is a way to say "Let's Start."
And making those resolutions
Is truly the first part.

Now maintenance will always be
The up-keep price to pay.
Well, January One is coming —
Get ready for that first day,

There will be a bonus
Do the work and you'll hear
It's one of life's great rewards —
'Twill be easier next year.

Resolution time

Have you ever tried the latest diet?
It's something a lot of us actually do.
I've stopped counting how many–
Of course I really don't know about you.

Being a vegetarian seems very popular.
Might as well give it a try.
It might be one of the healthy choices
And you don't have to give up pie.

Soon, however I found myself copying
"Where's the beef?" one woman Said.
Then I began to miss chicken-
Not enough to have eggs instead.

I've decided to become a "FLEXITARIAN",
Someone I know invented that word.
It means "To each his very own taste"
And that's the best diet I've ever heard.

New Year's Time Again ?

It's time to say Welcome
To a brand New Year.
The January resolutions
Are already here.

No learning "Chat Room" –
I like face to face.
If I had to Text,
I would lose the race.

Blondes have most fun;
Why ever go red?
I already sleep In –
And go Late to Bed.

There's always a diet
Too good to be true.
I'd cut spending in half –
But can't buy just One Shoe!

Good-bye to 2020.
I'll not shed a tear.
Deciding on changes?
Let's wait 'til Next Year!

It's Got To Be Love

It's funny about relationships,
They come in all sizes.
One thing is for sure –
They're full of surprises.

He may really be too short,
And she may be too tall,
But if you really care
It doesn't matter at all.

Of course, she's too young,
And he is much too old.
If you just reversed that,
The same thing will be told.

Love is a great mystery,
Not just set out in books.
In the eye of the beholder ?
Is that answer about looks?

The best glue may be humor.
It can usually save the day.
One oldster said it perfectly -
" I always let him have my way"

Love Is The First Step

Love is the first step,
And it's very easy to take.
It's the follow-up that's hard
And decides the "make or break."

Love takes a lot of effort
And a caring every day.
There really are no short cuts,
And the road can't be one-way.

If each person gives a lot–
Seventy percent comes to mind–
There'll be enough left over
To forge a tie to bind.

Love is quite the taskmaster
And helps to decide your fate.
It really takes a lifetime –
Just know the rewards are great!

Yes, love is just the start,
And another thing is true –
If you want to be "Lucky in Love,"
You'll find it's mostly up to you!

Sign Up Here!

If you need a retreat
If you want to get away,
Don't wait, do it now.
Opt for your very own day.

Don't put others on alert
They just might interfere.
If everyone knows nothing,
You have nothing to fear.

Get your gear together;
You can stash it out of sight
You'll then be prepared
When the time is just right.

Whatever is your pleasure,
Just go have a ball

Let'em read " Gone Fishing"
That sign says it all!

www.ingramcontent.com/pod-product-compliance
Lightning Source LLC
Chambersburg PA
CBHW070802050426
42452CB00012B/2464